Childhood Med

WALTHAM FOREST
PUBLIC LIBRARIES

20p

CENTRAL

REFERENCE LIBRARY

Childhood Medicines
When you need them & What they are

Neil Buchanan
Illustrated by Jack Newnham

PIATKUS

Acknowledgments

This book is dedicated to JOSEPH KELSO

The author is indebted to Professor T Sorrell, Drs R Hall, D Roberton, J Baird-Lambert, D Mackintosh, S O'Flaherty, G L Smith, H O Wooller; Mrs E Jandera, J Fetherston, G O'Flaherty, and Misses R Spencer, J Craig and J de Neef for having read and commented on the manuscript. I am also greatly indebted to my wife Denise for her continued assistance with the preparation of this book.

CHILDHOOD MEDICINES

First published in Great Britain in 1987 by
Judy Piatkus (Publishers) Ltd of
5 Windmill Street, London W1P 1HF

Copyright © text, Neil Buchanan 1987
Copyright © illustrations, Doubleday Australia 1987

All rights reserved, no part of this publication may be produced, stored in a retrieval system, transmitted in any form or by any means, electronic, mechanical, photocopying, recording or otherwise, without the prior permission in writing of the publishers.

British Library Cataloguing in Publication Data

Buchanan, Neil
   Childhood medicines.
   1. Drugs, Non-prescription——Great Britain
   I. Title
   615'.1'0941   RM671.5.G7

   ISBN 0-86188-649-6

Anglicisation by Dr. Lee Bond
Printed in Great Britain at
The Bath Press, Avon

Contents

Acknowledgments	4
Introduction	7
Understanding medicines	9
1 Childhood infections: how often and how many?	11
2 How are medicines made and marketed?	15
3 Children and medicines	21
4 Always keep medicines locked away	29
5 What is a prescription?	33
6 Antibiotics: why and when?	41
Common illnesses	49
7 Fever: what to do about it	51
8 Common infections	57
9 Persistent illnesses	67
10 Everyday maladies	73
11 Tummy troubles	77
12 Allergies	83
13 Urinary infections	87
14 Hyperactivity	91

Prevention	93
15 Immunisation: so very important	95
16 Vitamins: who needs them?	101
Epilogue	105
Appendices	107
1 Some questions that parents might ask	108
2 Common medicines used in childhood	117
3 What to keep in the medicine cabinet	123
4 Useful addresses	125
5 Further reading	126

Introduction

We all take medicines from time to time, whilst some of us need to take medication regularly. Over the last few years there has arisen a healthy concern in society about the usefulness and safety of drugs both prescribed by doctors and those obtained over the counter from pharmacists. This is particularly the case among parents, who are concerned about giving medication to their children. This has been compounded by the present trend towards so called 'natural' remedies.

The health profession is of course aware of this scepticism and concern. Many members of the profession are sympathetic while others find it irksome to be questioned about what they see as their territory. Parents often have the feeling that their doctor may find it easier to prescribe than to discuss their questions. Writing a prescription is really quite symbolic. If you think about it, when you go to the doctor, the writing of a prescription is the last thing which occurs during a consultation and the hidden meaning is 'the consultation is over'. This often leaves no time to discuss the prescribed medication; its value or side effects. This is even more the case for mothers of young children who may be fretful and crying, disturbing the peace and quiet of the doctor's surgery.

This book is designed to provide basic information for parents on medicines for their children. It is not an encyclopaedia of currently available drugs as these already exist. The book provides information on how the medicines that you get from the chemist are studied for safety, how they can best be given to children, when they really need to be given and so on. It also covers some general topics such as the management of fever, when to give antibiotics and the use of vitamins. More specific areas including the need for immunisation, the treatment of asthma, tummy troubles, coughs and colds, tonsillitis and ear infections are also discussed. It is neither possible, nor desirable, to separate medicines from illnesses and it is for this reason that both subjects are discussed.

These topics are discussed openly so as to highlight the fact that many of the decisions made by doctors are not simply black and white. They come in all shades of grey which are based on the latest information available, current prescribing trends, the doctor's own personal experience and such like. It has been designed to be a readable book which it is hoped will provide basic information for parents to allow them to discuss matters of medication for their children more fruitfully with their doctor.

The book is written as part of the health education programme of the Paediatric Health Education Unit of the University of Sydney based at the Westmead Hospital. The basic philosophy of the Unit is that well informed parents or patients are better able to cope with their illness and thus improve the quality of their lives and those of their children.

Understanding medicines

1 Childhood infections: how often and how many?

We all get ill from time to time, but in early childhood, parents often feel that their children have one illness after another. A common concern for parents is the repeated infections that children get. This is a common reason for consultation with general practitioners and paediatricians; 'My son always seems to have a cold or a sore throat'. For some parents, the three or four year old child never seems to be free of some minor illness or other and they spend many hours at the doctor's surgery. The numerous courses of antibiotics that children receive are also a source of concern to some parents, as they wonder if they are necessary and if they may not in fact be harmful when taken six or eight times a year.

Why young children get so many infections

At birth, the body's immune (defence) system is immature although the baby will have received some temporary resistance from antibodies passed on from the mother during pregnancy and breast-feeding. Antibodies are substances in the blood which help to fight infections. They are produced when the body comes into contact with an antigen, a substance which stimulates the formation of an antibody to that particular antigen. For example, if a child has mumps, he or she is infected with the mumps virus (the antigen) which stimulates the formation of an antibody. This mumps antibody persists in the blood stream for a long time and will help to prevent the child from getting mumps again.

However, with viral infections like influenza (flu) there are many different types of viruses and thus different antigens. So if a child had flu last year, he or she will have antibodies to last year's virus and antigen. If this year's virus has a different antigen, then those antibodies will not be effective. This explains why it is possible to get flu on many occasions.

Invading virus (antigen) stimulates the formation of antibody defence

Young children have few antibodies, so that when they first come into contact with bacteria or viruses of which there are many hundreds, they have little protection. However, once infected, they will develop antibodies and are unlikely to be ill with that particular virus again. This accounts for the large number of infections that young children have in the first few years of life. Many parents will have noticed that when their children first go to preschool or kindergarten, they seem to pick up a lot of coughs and colds. **This is quite normal, they are building up their body defences for the rest of their lives.** There are some children, although very few indeed, who are unable to make antibodies who have some other abnormality of their immune system. This is very rare and does not account for the ordinary repeated infections of childhood.

How many infections are normal?

Having suggested that repeated infections are both common and normal in childhood, how many are acceptable? Fortunately, due to the excellent work done at the Royal Children's Hospital in Melbourne, this can be explained. **A normal, healthy, average 12 year old can be expected to have had 67 infections during his or her life, 37 of these in the first six years.** These 37 infections may be composed of 17 minor colds, seven severe colds, three ear infections, six to seven other respiratory infections including an episode of croup and one of bronchitis, two episodes of diarrhoea and two skin infections. **This means that young children get quite a lot of infections and this is normal.**

The purpose of this chapter is not to suggest that you avoid taking your child to the doctor when he or she has an infection. It is purely aimed at introducing the idea that minor, recurrent infections are normal in childhood. If you go to your doctor, antibiotics are very likely to be prescribed. See Chapter 6 for more information about this. Blood tests may also be suggested. These could include a blood count to look at the white blood cells which are responsible for fighting infection or to look at the level of blood immunoglobulins which indicate a measure of the antibodies that we have spoken of. More sophisticated tests are available, but very rarely required.

2 How are medicines made and marketed?

As a result of the thalidomide tragedy, the more recent Debendox scare, problems with the Dalkon shield and the poisoning of Tylenol capsules in the USA, it is not surprising that the general public are concerned about the treatments that they may be given. This has led to an increased interest in how drugs are developed, tested for safety and subsequently marketed. This chapter, albeit briefly, discusses these matters.

How are drugs made?

Most new drugs (the terms medicines, medications and drugs are used here and all have the same meaning) are developed by pharmaceutical companies mainly in the USA, Europe and Japan. Many chemical substances are screened every year to see if they have any medical value. Of about 200,000 substances screened, probably only about 15 to 30 will ever be marketed. This gives you an idea of the difficulty and expense in developing new drugs.

When a chemical substance is thought to be of medical value, it is first tested in animals to find out possible hazards in humans and to obtain a rough idea of suitable dosage. The next step is to test out the drug on a small group of human volunteers; often the laboratory staff who are working on the development of the drug. Such information is then reviewed by the national Health Department of the country concerned, in Britain, the D.H.S.S. If the drug is judged to be potentially useful and safe, the pharmaceutical company then moves onto the next phase of larger scale studies in patients with the particular illness or illnesses for which the drug is to be used. These studies are usually done in teaching hospitals with the involvement of university and hospital staff, under strict supervision. The patients treated in these studies must give their consent in writing to be involved in what is, after all, an experiment. Sometimes the studies may take several years, and involve the treatment of several thousand patients.

All the information obtained on the drug is then compiled by the pharmaceutical company and submitted to the Department of Health and Social Security. The results are scrutinised by the Department and by independent experts, a process which may take another one to two years. If this final assessment is satisfactory, the company will then receive permission to market and advertise the drug for the specific purpose for which it was developed. Even this laborious process, designed for maximum safety, will not pick up each and every side effect. Doctors have a responsibility to report drug side effects, especially with new drugs and the D.H.S.S. should continue ongoing surveillance for any problems.

Why drugs cost so much

It is because it takes such a very long time to get drugs onto the market that they are so expensive. It may cost a drug company, for example, 50 to 100 million dollars to develop a particular drug. Drug development is done by the major ethical pharmaceutical companies who obviously need to cover their costs and make a profit for further research and development. These companies are called ethical companies because their research is based on codes of ethics which dictate how experiments should be conducted on animals and humans. The

companies need to recoup the enormous cost of development of each drug and to finance research into new compounds. Patent protection on a drug lasts 16 years from the time of discovery and at least half of this time may have passed before the drug is approved for marketing.

When the patent runs out the company may seek a patent extension. However, what happens more often, especially if the drug is successful, is that a pharmaceutical company not involved in basic research will begin to produce the drug under another brand name. The same strict requirements apply and the new manufacturer's product has to be shown to the satisfaction of the Committee on Safety of Medicines (within the D.H.S.S.) to be as good as the original drug. Compared to new drug development this is easy to do and involves little expense. Thus these products may be considerably cheaper than the original drug.

The naming of drugs

All drugs have at least two names and this is often confusing to patients. First there is a generic name which describes the active ingredient of the drug and then there is the brand name (trade name) which is the name given by the manufacturer to the drug. Thus while there is usually only one generic name, there may be any number of brand names. For example, paracetamol, which is a generic name, is often recognised by its trade names, Panadol or Calpol.

The advantage of generic prescribing (i.e. prescribing by generic name rather than trade name) is often cheaper medication. This is because, as mentioned previously, the company which manufactures a drug that has already been developed, does not have the expense of researching that particular drug and can sell it more cheaply than the original company can. So, for example, if your doctor prescribes a generic name then you have the choice of either the original drug (which will be more expensive) or the newer drug (which will be cheaper). The disadvantages are that the newer generic product may not work in exactly the same way in the body and in the longer term if the original companies that do the research cannot make money out of their products, their research will cease. This would be unfortunate for all of us.

3 Children and medicines

Many, indeed most, children's illnesses are relatively brief and self limiting. In other words, they last for a few days and then settle down. As opposed to adults, who as the years go by develop chronic illnesses and need to be on regular medication, most children have acute episodes of illness and need intermittent medication. Of course some children have chronic illnesses but fortunately most don't fall into this category. As a result, children tend to take much less medication than adults and in addition, the drugs which they take are often relatively simple agents, mainly antibiotics, and antipyretics (medicines used to reduce fever). Childhood medicines come in a variety of forms.

Tablets

These are the commonest form in which drugs are available. A tablet consists of the active ingredient surrounded by harmless substances which bind the active substance together. Very young children are unable to swallow tablets, although it may be possible to crush them and mix the fragments with jam or honey in a spoon. Sometimes crushing a tablet disturbs the absorption of the active ingredient from the stomach but according to the manufacturers there are very few tablets which are not able to be crushed. Those that are better not crushed include the slow release theophylline compounds used to treat asthma such as Nuelin SA and TheoDur.

Usually, once the tablet is swallowed, it reaches the stomach where it dissolves and is absorbed into the blood stream. Once in the blood stream the drug is carried around the body and goes out of the blood stream into the body tissues. Many drugs are broken down by the liver and excreted from the body by the kidneys into the urine.

Capsules

Some medications are presented in capsule form although few are made for children, mostly because they are large and difficult for children to swallow.

Liquid forms

There are two liquid forms of medication, suspensions and elixirs. **Suspensions** are solutions where the drug is suspended in a liquid. For example, Amoxil or Septrin. These need to be shaken well before use otherwise the active ingredient may sit at the bottom of the bottle.

Elixirs are solutions in which the active ingredient is dissolved in the liquid which is water, but may contain other substances such as alcohol. Elixirs are clear liquids and do not need to be shaken with the same vigour as suspensions. The best known elixir is Phenergan.

Most liquid drug forms contain sweet flavourings to make them more palatable and in general, this makes them quite appealing to children. However, the sweeteners in these medications are a source of concern as if children take them often, they may develop dental caries.

Children and medicines

Different ways of giving medication

Inhaled medications

The treatment of asthma in particular has been revolutionised by the advent of inhaled medications. There are now numerous inhaler devices which deliver the medication directly to the airways and lungs where they are needed. Inhaled drugs are hardly absorbed into the blood stream and so are very safe and produce few side effects.

Suppositories

These are little wax based, rocket shaped objects which are put into the rectum (back passage). This way of giving drugs is very popular in Latin countries, but much less so in the Anglo-Saxon world. Whilst many drugs can be administered by this route, absorption into the blood stream is not always reliable. In children, suppositories may be useful in the management of fever, stopping convulsions and in the management of constipation.

Injectable forms

These are sterile preparations of the drug either in a powder form or already dissolved. They can be injected either into a vein (intravenously), under the skin (subcutaneously) or into a muscle (intramuscularly). Obviously if a drug is injected intravenously it goes directly into the bloodstream and avoids the need to be absorbed from the stomach, so that it acts much more rapidly. Intravenous injections are given to people who need urgent treatment, and would be used, for example, to give antibiotics in meningitis or theophylline to children with a bad attack of asthma.

Getting a child to take medication

It can sometimes be difficult to get a child to take medication. Quite often this is because they are frightened of having something foreign put in their mouth with a big adult leaning over them or because they do not like the taste of the medication. There are no easy ways to get around this problem and most families develop their own tricks for getting their children to take medication.

From a practical point of view, almost all medications can be taken with meals. There are only a handful of drugs that must be taken on an empty stomach and none of them, with the exception of the penicillins, e.g. Amoxil, are commonly used in children.

Taking medicines with meals has two advantages. Firstly it lessens any stomach upsets that may occur with the drug and secondly it makes sense to pop a pill in one's mouth when it is already open for a more enjoyable purpose. Most medicines given to children are taken three times a day, quite a few twice a day (especially in chronic conditions) and rarely are they needed four times a day. The concept of four times a day medication, in other words every six hours, is quite illogical as few parents would be willing to wake a sleeping child at 2 am to do battle with their medication.

The importance of taking prescribed medication

This leads on to the subject of **compliance** which means how reliably a person takes his or her medication. Doctors often talk of 'noncompliance', in other words how often medications, or doses, are not taken. In an ideal world, patients would follow their doctor's instructions and finish the medicine prescribed for them. This of course does not happen. The importance of this depends on whether it is an acute or a chronic illness. In an acute illness such as a sore throat, which will get better in a couple of days whatever is done, medication may be prescribed for five to ten days. Very few adults, let alone children, finish such a course of treatment, because as soon as they feel well, the need to take the medication fades. In the real world, as opposed to an ideal one, most of us behave this way and survive, so it seems a reasonable rule of thumb. On the other hand if a child has a urinary tract infection which could lead to kidney damage if not adequately treated, it is important that the prescribed course of medication be completed, even if the symptoms have gone. This should be clearly explained by the doctor and reinforced by the pharmacist.

In children and adults with a chronic condition such as asthma, epilepsy, high blood pressure or diabetes, compliance is essential to lessen the effects of the disease. It is important for the patient and the parents to find out as much as possible about the medication that is being prescribed and to ask the following sorts of questions.

- Why are they taking the medication?
- What benefits can be expected from the drug? Is it really necessary or is the illness going to settle down anyway?
- How long are they expected to take it?
- How often should they take it and what happens if they vary the intervals?
- What are the side effects?
- Does it mix safely with anything else they may be taking?

All medicines have the potential to produce side effects to a greater or lesser extent. The occurrence of side effects depends on the drug itself and on the individual patient. We are all made up differently, so one person can take a drug quite happily while someone else may react to it. Some side effects can be predicted because they occur commonly, for example, when first starting a patient on drugs for the treatment of epilepsy, drowsiness is very common. They should be informed that this will last a week or so and then wear off. Other side effects are quite unpredictable. **You should always ask your doctor and pharmacist about side effects.** They should tell you of the common side effects but obviously will not mention all the rare ones which almost never occur. If your doctor or pharmacist are disinclined to discuss these matters with you, perhaps it is time for a change.

What is the role of the pharmacist in advising on healthcare?

Pharmacists do not get a great deal of training in this area and largely learn on the job. There is nothing wrong with this practical approach. In years gone by, when pharmacists were mainly dispensing chemists, they seemed to spend a lot of time with their clients and were frequently asked for advice on minor, and sometimes, major issues. With the advent of much more commercial chemist shops, a lot of this personal service has vanished although there is a move to enhance this in pharmacy practice. It is always worth having a chat with your pharmacist about the medicine that you are obtaining for yourself or your child. Pharmacists are also the best informed members of the community on over the counter medications (those that can be obtained without a prescription) and are very helpful in this regard.

4 Always keep medicines locked away

Medicines and household products insecurely stored are a hazard to young children. Every year many children are brought to hospital as a result of accidental poisoning. Often this is 'suspected' poisoning, because quite a lot of children who are brought to hospital with a story of being found with some medication or household product around them have in fact not actually swallowed any of it.

Children seem to end up in hospital through accidental poisoning because of curiosity, and this is especially true of toddlers. Nicely coloured, sugar coated pills look very much like Smarties! The main cause of poisoning is insecurely stored medication and household products.

Most accidental poisonings occur in the child's own home and the products swallowed are most often medicines, and less often, household agents. Obviously the exact nature of these products varies according to what is fashionable in the home or what is currently being prescribed. Common medicines include tranquillizers, antihistamines, antidepressants, barbiturates, antiepileptic drugs, aspirin, iron and so on. Particularly susceptible household products include turpentine, paraffin, bleach, poison baits, disinfectant, alcohol and many others.

In reality, most children who are suspected of swallowing, or who have swallowed a poison come to no harm. However, it is very frightening for parents to find their children in a puddle of paraffin or in a mound of tranquillizers. What to do in this situation?

- If the child is obviously unwell, drowsy or unconscious, call an ambulance or go straight to the closest hospital. Take a sample of what has been swallowed with you. It is a good idea to try and estimate the number of tablets swallowed.
- If the child is well and playful, as is so often the case, telephone your doctor, local hospital or Poisons Centre. Mention the age of the child, what he or she may have taken and if possible, how long ago the poison was taken. They will advise you on the next move.
- If in doubt, go to your closest hospital.

If you go to a hospital, what might happen? This will depend upon what has been swallowed, for example, ingestion of medication will usually warrant admission, if only for observation. This is less likely to happen with household products. If the poison was taken within three to four hours of getting to hospital, the child will probably be given some Syrup of Ipecac (ipecacuanha), which will make him vomit to bring the poison up. This may be repeated once. If that is not successful, it may be necessary to try and get the poison up by passing a tube down the gullet and washing out the stomach. Making the child vomit, or washing out the stomach, should not be done if the child is very drowsy, or if paraffin or corrosives have been swallowed. Activated charcoal may also be given either by mouth or down the tube, as it binds the poison in the intestines and prevents it from being absorbed. Some children will need specific treatment for their poisoning, but most will simply be admitted overnight for observation. This is often very useful, as parents feel guilty that their child has been poisoned and the security of hospital observation allows time for emotions to settle down.

Always keep medicines locked away 31

Interestingly, and sadly, despite feelings of guilt, it has been shown that very few parents, when they get home, try to remedy the situation by securely storing medicines and household products. There have been a number of public education campaigns employed to try to reduce the incidence of poisoning; most have been unsuccessful. **It is very much an attitude of 'It won't happen to us'!**

Some practical hints to prevent your child swallowing poison include:

- Keeping medicines **locked** in a cupboard.
- Storing dangerous household products well out of the child's reach; preferably in a securely fastened cupboard.
- Pouring cleaning products down the drain or toilet after use; washing out the container and then discarding it.
- Always reading the label on the bottle before taking or giving medicine.
- Keeping all substances in their original containers. Do not for example put paraffin in old cold drink bottles.

DOCTOR:
(Wizard of medicine)

PRESCRIPTION:
(Magic formula to make it better)

'ORDINARY' PERSONS

5 What is a prescription?

A prescription is a document which allows you to go to a pharmacy and obtain the medication prescribed. On the prescription is information from the doctor to the pharmacist as to what medication has been prescribed, the dosage and the length of treatment.

Prescriptions are notoriously difficult to read and pharmacists among other skills, have to become experts at deciphering handwriting. Before discussing what is actually on a prescription, it is worth pointing out that in most countries there are two types of prescriptions:

- A standard issue N.H.S. prescription which is used for medications that have been approved for a government subsidy. These are medications which in the main are seen as being essential for treatment of a particular condition.

- Prescriptions written on a doctor's own notepaper, which are for medications not on the government subsidised list. This does not mean that there is anything wrong with these medications, but that in the opinion of a committee of experts employed by the government, these medications have no advantage either in cost or efficacy, over those already on the subsidised list. It may also be that the medications are cheaper than the patient contribution and therefore do not qualify for a subsidy.

What is actually written on a prescription? Two examples, one on a government prescription and one on notepaper, are shown:

Pharmacy Stamp	NATIONAL HEALTH SERVICE	FORM FP10(HP) (Revised 3/84)

SURNAME Mr/Mrs/Miss MANDY JONES

Age if under 12 years

initials and one full forename

Address 24 PENNY LANE LONDON N.18

Pharmacist's pack & quantity endorsement	No. of days treatment N.B. Ensure dose is stated	NP	Pricing Office use only

Tetracycline 250 mg
T b.d.

Signature of Doctor

Date 18.12.86

Doctor's Name and Initials in Block Letters

For Pharmacist | Name of District or BG. Name and Address of Hospital or Clinic and Institution Code

SPECIMEN ONLY

No. of prescns. on form.

IMPORTANT: Read Notes overleaf before going to the pharmacy

M 483851

What is a prescription?

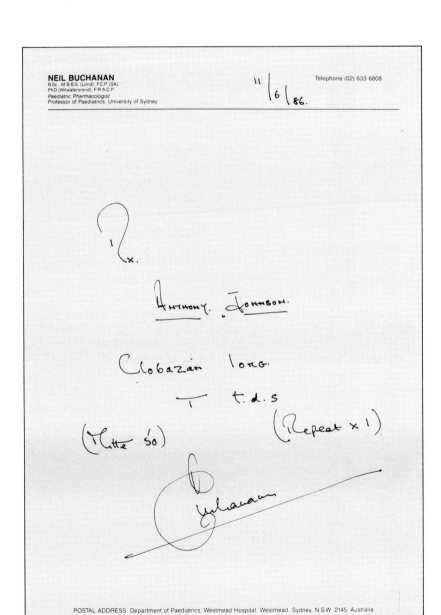

The N.H.S. prescription

This is a prescription for an adolescent girl with acne, who requires a course of the antibiotic Tetracycline. It bears the prescriber's and the patient's name and address as well as the date. It then specifies the drug, in this case Tetracycline and the dosage of the drug (250 milligrams per dose). Below that is a T which means one capsule/tablet followed by the term b.d., which is short for 'bis in diem' which means twice daily. This is then followed by the doctor's signature.

The private prescription

This prescription is for a medication not N.H.S. approved, which is used for the treatment of anxiety and may be used to treat epilepsy. The first part of the prescription 'Rx' means literally 'Take thou' or recipe or superscription. It means in practice 'this is the treatment prescribed'. Thereafter the drug is named, in this case clobazam, followed by the recommended dosage, the number of tablets T (one at a time) to be taken three times daily (t.d.s.). Below that on the left, is an expression (Mitte 50) which means the number of tablets that the pharmacist can legally give out for any one prescription and on the right, that the prescription can be repeated once by the pharmacist without the patient seeing a doctor again. This is then signed by the doctor. Such a prescription will be on the doctor's private stationery.

What is a prescription?

There are a number of other abbreviations which appear on prescriptions which are explained in the table below.

A guide to prescription shorthand

Ad lib	As desired (take whenever you feel like it)
b.d. (b.i.d.)	Bis in diem; twice daily
cap(s)	Capsule(s)
g	Gram(me) = 1000 milligrams
mane	To be taken in the mornings
mg	Milligram = 1/1000 of a gram(me)
ml	Millilitre
nocte	To be taken at night
p.o.	Per os; take by mouth
p.r.n	Pro re nata; take as the occasion arises
q3h	Take every 3 hours
q.i.d.	Take 4 times daily
t.d.s. (t.i.d.)	Take 3 times daily
µg	Microgram; mcg = 1/1000 of a milligram
Ī	On a prescription, means take one tablet/capsule
ĪĪ	On a prescription, means take two tablets/capsules
ĪĪĪ	On a prescription, means take three tablets/capsules

The symbolism of a prescription

The other aspect of the prescription is its symbolism. Think of the average consultation. When you go to see the doctor, he or she will listen to what you have to tell them and may ask some questions, then you will be examined either totally or in the part of the body where the problem appears to be. This may take ten or 15 minutes. Then out comes the prescription pad, a quick squiggle and the prescription is handed to you. The handing over of the prescription has come to mean that the consultation is over, 'pick up your bed and walk!'. If you watch consultations as an observer, it is not uncommon to see patients begin to get up as soon as the prescription is written; they know that the end of the consultation has come. This is regrettable as most people keep any questions they might have until the end of a consultation and thus feel inhibited about starting a new conversation.

When you get a prescription from your doctor, if it has not been explained to your satisfaction, ask about it. You should know:

- The name of the medication being prescribed

- What it is for

- What it can be expected to do

- What its side effects are

- How long it should be taken for

Don't be afraid to ask. After all, it is in your best interests to know exactly what is happening.

What is a prescription?

6 Antibiotics: why and when?

The use, or perhaps overuse, of antibiotics is a controversial topic and one which parents find confusing. It is very common for a paediatrician to be asked, 'John has had so many courses of antibiotics, surely that can't be good for him?' The dilemma which surrounds the use of antibiotics in the community is discussed in this chapter. However, it does not apply to antibiotic use for the ill patient in hospital.

What are antibiotics?

Antibiotics, otherwise known as antimicrobial (against microbes) agents are effective in treating diseases caused by bacteria. They are of no value in treating illnesses caused by viruses. What is the difference between bacteria and viruses? Bacteria are single celled microbes which reproduce by dividing, sometimes very rapidly. A disease may be caused either by the harmful bacteria themselves damaging your tissues or by poisons (toxins) which they produce. Bacterial diseases include tonsillitis, boils, some kinds of food poisoning, whooping cough, pneumonia and tuberculosis amongst others. Viruses are the smallest microbes and they can only grow inside living cells. They invade the cells and use the resources of the cell to multiply. This damages the cells and produces the symptoms of illness. Many illnesses are viral including colds, influenza, measles, poliomyelitis, chicken pox, mumps, rubella and so on.

Why do doctors sometimes prescribe antibiotics for viruses?

There is a lot of development in the field of drugs to deal with viruses, but at present this is at an experimental stage. So antibiotics should only be used to treat infections caused by bacteria. Yet you may wonder why sometimes when you go to a doctor you may be told 'It's a viral infection, but I will give you an antibiotic' or 'It's a sore throat, so I would suggest an antibiotic'. If the infection is due to a virus, antibiotics will not help. The problem is that it is usually not possible to be absolutely certain whether an infection is due to a virus or a bacteria.

Antibiotics: why and when?

The only way to know with certainty is by doing blood tests or taking swabs from the throat and trying to grow the bacteria or identify the virus. These tests often take several days. During this time the patient will either get better or may get worse. It is this dilemma which makes doctors prescribe antibiotics so freely.

Over prescription or not

Teaching hospital doctors have argued over the years that general practitioners over prescribe antibiotics which are unnecessary, and which may produce more side effects than are warranted. They are also concerned that this overuse may cause certain bacteria to become resistant to the drugs. The general practitioners have responded by saying that they do not have the security of a hospital laboratory to help them, they cannot have the patient under their eye in hospital for observation and that if they do not prescribe antibiotics, the patient will go elsewhere to get them.

There are rights and wrongs on both sides of this argument which is likely to last for some years. The reality of the situation is that in childhood just under half of the sore throats and chest infections are due to bacteria, whilst probably about 80 per cent of ear infections are due to bacteria. Urinary infections are nearly always bacterial and so should be treated with antibiotics.

Efforts to encourage general practitioners to prescribe fewer antibiotics have had limited results. The reasons for this have already been mentioned but there is also the influence of the pharmaceutical industry to be taken into account. The pharmaceutical industry is in business to provide healthcare products and to make money. Thus they will encourage the general practitioner, in particular, and other doctors, to prescribe their particular product. Especially the latest, fanciest and probably most expensive antibiotic. This is part and parcel of a free enterprise economy.

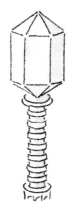

A type of virus
magnified 225,000 times

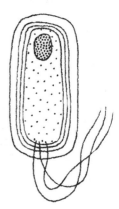

A type of bacteria
magnified 30,000 times

How your doctor chooses an antibiotic

So you can see that there are a number of factors, some commercial, which relate to the use of antibiotics. Having said this, you are still probably wondering how your doctor chooses an antibiotic for your child's particular illness. Again, there are a number of factors which come into making this decision. These include:

What the illness is: It is known which bacteria are involved in causing most cases of tonsillitis or otitis media (middle ear infection), so that an antibiotic can be prescribed without doing any tests.

Whether your child is allergic to a particular antibiotic: If so, it should be avoided. For example penicillin should be avoided by those who have had an allergic response when given the drug previously.

Which is the cheapest, yet effective, antibiotic:

Whether the antibiotic will mix all right in the body with any other medications that your child is taking: For example if your child has asthma and is taking theophylline (e.g. Nuelin), the antibiotic Erythromycin should not be prescribed as it will change the way that theophylline is handled in the body and may produce theophylline intoxication.

Bacteria and antibiotics

There are lots of different types of bacteria, and these can be divided into two broad groups: so called Gram positive and Gram negative bacteria. The term Gram refers to the use of the Gram stain, a chemical way of differentiating between the two groups of bacteria. Some antibiotics are mainly of use for Gram positive bacteria and others for Gram negative infections. However there is a group of antibiotics called 'broad spectrum' antibiotics which are useful in treating both groups of bacteria. It is these 'broad spectrum' antibiotics which are so widely prescribed on the basis that they will deal with most things most of the time. Of these types of antibiotics, the drug Amoxil would be the best known.

If we accept that there is a degree of overprescribing, does it matter? The possible advantages are that infections will be nipped in the bud and complications will be lessened. There is some evidence for this, as in this day and age, meningitis is relatively uncommon and the complications of otitis media such as mastoiditis (infection of the mastoid air cells behind the ear) are rarely seen. The advantage for the doctor is that it makes him or her feel more secure because something has been done to alleviate the illness.

The disadvantages are that, as a matter of principle, medications should not be prescribed unless they are really needed. As taxpayers we are paying for the unnecessary prescriptions and drug side effects do occur. Although antibiotic side effects are not very common, it is irritating enough to develop side effects if you really need the medication but even more so if it was not really essential.

This chapter has not answered the question as to the rights and wrongs of antibiotic prescribing. It has attempted to provide you as parents, and perhaps patients yourselves, with information as to why the situation is as it is.

It is up to you to ask your doctor:

• Why an antibiotic is being prescribed

• Is it really necessary?

• Will your child get better without antibiotics?

• Whether there are any side effects of the medication

Common illnesses

7 Fever: what to do about it

Considering that fever is the commonest of all childhood symptoms, it is surprising that the understanding of fever and how best to deal with it remain somewhat controversial. Fever is a common accompaniment to all childhood infections, and, in simple terms, is one of the body's responses to the infection.

Is fever harmful?

The answer to this fundamental question is almost certainly NO. It may be uncomfortable and unpleasant but not dangerous. Perhaps for children who are prone to febrile convulsions, it could be considered potentially dangerous. There is no absolute figure for when fever is considered to be potentially harmful and opinions range from temperatures that are in the vicinity of 41-43°C (106-110°F). Some people argue that fever is beneficial as it is a normal body reaction to infection which stimulates the body's defence mechanisms to deal with the infection.

Confusion arises because of parental views on fever. There have been many studies in this area and all have produced very much the same result. The confusion revolves around a misunderstanding of the dangers of fever, what the normal body temperature is, how often to take the temperature in an ill child and how best to manage fever.

Symptoms of fever

The normal body temperature is 37°C (98.4°F). Most children with a fever will be unwell and off colour. Just by putting a hand on the forehead it may well be possible to assess whether the child is unduly hot. This is best followed by measuring the temperature with a thermometer in the mouth or in the armpit. Leave the thermometer in place for a good two minutes.

The strip like thermometers which can be placed on the forehead are sometimes unreliable and cannot be recommended.

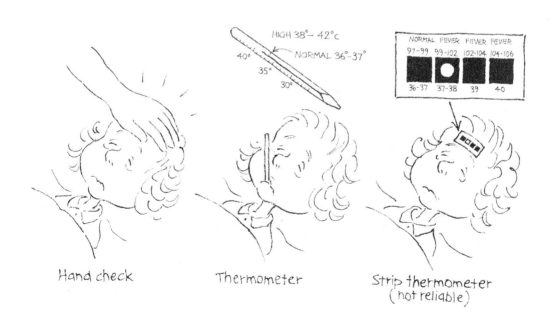

Hand check   Thermometer   Strip thermometer
                                     (not reliable)

What to do

Having ascertained that the child has a fever, what next? If the child seems reasonably well, it may not be necessary to do anything at all. He or she may just have a passing viral infection which will last a day or two and wear off. If the child is unwell, unduly irritable, refusing feeds, in pain or has had febrile convulsions in the past then treatment should be considered.

Making the child comfortable: We all know that when we are feverish we feel grumpy and uncomfortable. Often we want to go off to bed and sleep. Just getting comfortable is a big help. The same applies for children. Get the child to bed or lying comfortably somewhere else in the house.

Provide plenty of fluids, either water, ice blocks or cold drinks because a fever will make the child perspire and lose fluid. It also helps to bring the fever down a little bit by avoiding dehydration.

Be more attentive to the child than usual and perhaps get some new books, colouring in books, toys, and so on, relative to their age.

Take the temperature from time to time to see how things are going if you feel this to be necessary. Don't do this every hour; it does not help and just disturbs and irritates the child.

Cool the child down: Avoid having too much clothing on the child and keep bed linen to a minimum. Sponging children has not been proven to help reduce a fever but it has been shown to be comforting, which in itself may be worthwhile. Cold or iced water should be avoided, as this will cool the skin and prevent heat loss through the skin which in turn makes the temperature within the body rise, and this is what you're hoping to avoid.

Sponging with tepid water (about body temperature, 37°C) is suggested.

Medicine for the fever: In 1986, the Committee on Safety of Medicines, having considered the evidence on links between an unpleasant liver disease called Reye's syndrome and the use of aspirin, has recommended that aspirin should no longer be given to children under 12 years. This has left one medicine only suitable for the treatment of fever in children (e.g. Panadol, Calpol).

Working out the cause of the fever

As already mentioned, the fever is due to an infection. It may be just a viral sore throat which will settle down in a couple of days. On the other hand it may be due to an ear infection, in which case the child is likely to complain of pain in the ear and may need antibiotics to resolve the problem.

When to contact the doctor

When to contact your doctor is a matter of common sense. If the child looks reasonably well, then treatment at home would be ample. If on the other hand the fever gets worse, the child is quite unwell or there is some other reason for concern, contact your doctor.

8 Common infections

As discussed in Chapter 1, children will have a number of minor illnesses during their childhood. While this is normal, some of these may need treating. This chapter tells you about some of the more typical infections that your child is likely to have.

Coughs and colds

We all know what coughs and colds are about as we have all had them from time to time. We also know that they get better in a couple of days whatever is done about them. Those couple of days may not be all that cheerful, but they do come to an end.

What you may not realise is that coughs and colds are caused almost exclusively by viruses and so do not need antibiotics! Most of us when we have a cold take an aspirin or two for the general discomfort and wait for it to settle down. For children, as discussed in Chapter 7, it is better to use paracetamol which will have the same effect.

What about nose drops or sprays and antihistamines? There is certainly no need to use nose drops or sprays in this situation as the cold will only last for a day or two. Occasionally in small babies, nose drops will help to clear a very blocked nose. The chronic, or recurrent, use of nasal preparations can cause a serious nasal problem, so this practice should be avoided. Antihistamines, of which there are many, e.g. Phenergan, are sometimes prescribed to dry up secretions from a runny nose. However, for a start, they are not very effective and secondly they may make the child quite drowsy. They also have side effects such as overactivity and nightmares, which children are somewhat prone to and so should be avoided unless really needed. They are not needed for the common cold, although they may help in people who suffer from hay fever.

Sore throats

A sore throat is exactly what the name suggests, a sore, red throat which is inflamed leading to discomfort, especially on swallowing. There may be an associated fever and the child may complain of pain in the ear, which is pain referred from the throat. Sore throats are usually due to viruses, so antibiotics are rarely needed. Paracetamol is useful for the pain and discomfort.

Tonsillitis

Tonsillitis means an infection of the tonsils. This may be associated with fever, bad breath, pain on swallowing and swelling of the glands (lymph glands) under the jaw.

Tonsillitis is usually due to bacteria, especially if flecks of pus are visible on the tonsils. As there is a reasonable chance that the infection is bacterial in nature, most doctors would prescribe an antibiotic such as Amoxil, Septrin Ceclor, Bactrim. Don't forget that the child is uncomfortable and feverish, so paracetamol may be helpful.

What about tonsillitis and antibiotics?

Tonsillitis is a good example of the compliance issue that was discussed in Chapter 3. Your doctor may prescribe an antibiotic for five to ten days. In most cases the child will be fine in two to three days. Should you go on with the antibiotics? There are a number of theoretical reasons why you should, but the reality is that you are unlikely to do so, especially as when the child feels better, he or she is even less likely to want to take the medication. It is quite uncommon for problems to return if treatment is stopped once the child is better, even if this is after only two to three days.

Should tonsils be taken out?

It is not possible to touch on the topic of tonsillitis without briefly mentioning the issue of tonsillectomy (taking the tonsils out). It is uncertain what the tonsils actually do, but it is known that they are part of the body's defence mechanism and presumably perform some useful function. Therefore, they should not be removed without good reason. If your child suffers from any of the following then a tonsillectomy might be worth considering.

- Repeated attacks of tonsillitis; at least three episodes of tonsillitis a year for two or more years.
- Chronic tonsillitis; seen in older children and adults.
- An abscess around the tonsils (quinsy).
- Obstruction of the breathing from massive tonsils.

Vague symptoms like feeling unwell, bad breath, not growing adequately and so on are no reason for having tonsils taken out. If a tonsillectomy is suggested for one of your children and you have any doubts about it, seek a second specialist opinion.

Parents are often loath to get a second opinion which is unfortunate because a second opinion can often help you make a decision you feel happy about. It is not a slight on your doctor to obtain a second opinion, you are purely exercising your right to clarify the situation to your satisfaction.

Ear problems

Middle ear infections: The commonest ear problem is an infection of the middle ear (otitis media). This is an infection, usually due to bacteria, in the middle ear, which lies behind the eardrum. When your doctor looks into your child's ear with an auroscope, he can see the drum. In otitis media the drum is red and often bulging outward; this is because of fluid or pus which has accumulated behind the drum. On the likely presumption that otitis media is a bacterial infection, antibiotics such as those suggested for tonsillitis, are usually prescribed. Paracetamol is recommended for pain and fever. If no treatment is given, the infection may either settle down on its own, become chronic or the drum may rupture with pus coming out of the ear. Sometimes, but rarely these days, it may be necessary to let the pus out by surgically making a small hole in the ear drum (myringotomy). Ear drops are of no value and if the drum has ruptured they may be harmful as they will actually get into the middle ear.

Glue ear: This is a collection of sticky fluid behind the drum, in the middle ear, which stops the little bones in the middle ear which transmit sound from moving normally. As a result, hearing is affected. The hearing loss is often quite subtle and may be present with inattention at home or at school. The cause of glue ear is uncertain and treatment consists of surgically inserting little ventilating tubes (grommets) through the ear drum into the middle ear, to let the fluid drain out. Although this treatment is believed to be correct it has not been absolutely proven to be of value.

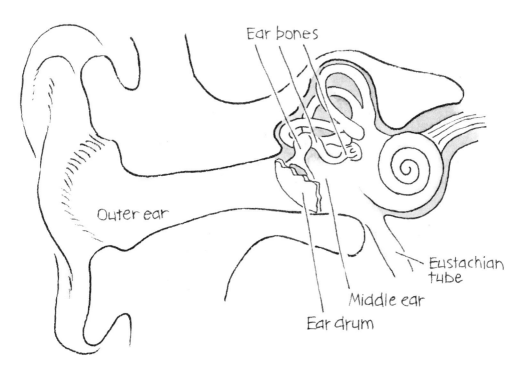

Chicken pox (Varicella)

This is a very contagious disease which children between the ages of five to ten often contract. It is caused by a viral infection with varicella zoster, the same virus that causes shingles in adults.

The incubation period is from ten to 21 days and the first symptoms are those of a rash, which may be very itchy. It begins as small red spots on the trunk. Quite rapidly the spots become larger, fluid filled blisters and spread from the trunk to the face, scalp, arms and legs. Over the next few days the blisters fill with pus, burst and form a scab. New spots may appear over about four days. The rash may sometimes affect the eyes, the mouth, the vagina and the rectum. Complete recovery takes about two weeks. For the most part complications are uncommon, although occasionally the blisters can become infected. Children should be encouraged not to scratch the blisters because of infection which in turn can leave a scar.

There is no specific treatment for chicken pox as it is a viral infection. A soothing lotion such as calamine lotion reduces the itch. Warm baths are helpful as they also reduce the itch and lessen the chance of the blisters getting infected. Fever should be treated with paracetamol. Aspirin should be avoided because of the association with Reye's Syndrome (see Chapter 7). There is presently no suitable vaccine to prevent chicken pox although this is being worked on.

Measles (Rubeola)

This is a contagious disease which affects the respiratory system, skin and the eyes. It is caused by the measles virus and has an incubation period of about ten days.

Common infections

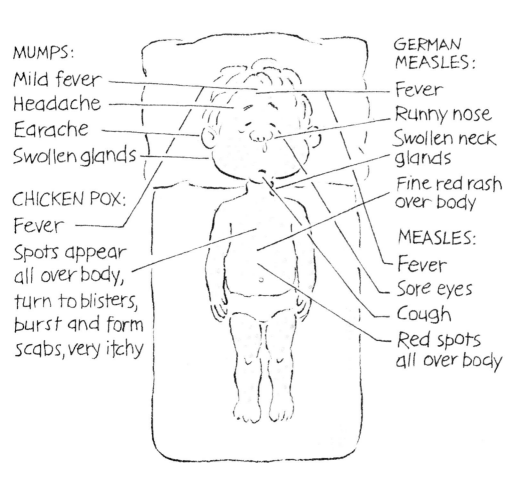

The spots, rashes and lumps of childhood

In most developed countries measles is perceived as a mild disease and this has led to a very low incidence of immunisation against it. This is unfortunate as measles can be quite an unpleasant illness with a number of complications. In developing countries, particularly in association with malnutrition, measles remains a major killer of children.

Symptoms consist of the features of a cold associated with a barking cough and fever. After a couple of days the eyes become red, sore and very sensitive to light. When the fever settles, red spots with little white centres (Koplik's spots) appear in the mouth. The fever then rises again and a rash appears on the face, neck, behind the ears and then spreads to the rest of the body. The rash often turns bright red, then brown and subsequently fades. The whole process takes about ten days.

Complications include middle ear infection, bronchitis, laryngitis, pneumonia and, on very rare occasions, infection of the brain (encephalitis). An equally rare complication which can occur some years after the illness is a degenerative condition of the brain called subacute sclerosing panencephalitis (SSPE). But it should be stressed that this is very rare indeed.

As measles is a viral infection there is no specific treatment. Of course the illness can be specifically prevented by immunisation. Treatment consists of paracetamol for the fever, calamine lotion for any itchy areas of the rash and darkening of the room if the eyes are sore. Antibiotics may be needed if complications arise.

Mumps

This is a contagious illness, due to the mumps virus, which usually occurs before 15 years of age. The main features are a mild fever, headache and earache. These are followed by swelling of the salivary glands, usually on one side of the face, and then a day or so later by swelling on the other side. There may also be swelling of the testicles (orchitis), the ovaries (oophoritis), the pancreas (pancreatitis) and very occasionally the brain (encephalitis).

Unfortunately, there is no specific treatment, although paracetamol may be helpful for pain and fever and cold compresses to the face may reduce the pain from the swollen salivary glands.

German Measles (Rubella)

This is a contagious viral infection which produces a mild illness. The concern about rubella is that if it is contracted by pregnant women in the first few weeks of pregnancy, it may cause abnormalities in the foetus (unborn child). It is for this reason that all secondary school girls are immunised against rubella.

Symptoms consist of fever, a runny nose, swollen neck glands and then about two days later a fine red rash on the face and neck. The rash then spreads to the body as a whole. The whole illness lasts about a week.

Being a mild illness little treatment is required, although paracetamol may be useful for the fever.

9 Persistent illnesses

Asthma

Asthma is an important condition in childhood. About one in seven children will have an attack of asthma at some time or other. Despite its importance, asthma will only be briefly discussed as the subject has been covered in detail in *Childhood Asthma* by the same author. Interested readers are referred to that book.

The important messages to get across with regard to asthma are first, it is common, second, many children will grow out of it as they get older and third, the medications available for the treatment of asthma are both very effective and safe.

Treatment may consist of medications taken by mouth (orally) which can be in either liquid form or tablets. There are also some so called slow release preparations available such as Nuelin SA and TheoDur, which because of the way the tablets are made up, need to be taken only twice a day. Perhaps the biggest advance over the past few years has been the development of a number of medications that can be inhaled. As we discussed in Chapter 3, this has the advantage of delivering the medications are also very safe. They can be delivered with either puffer devices, inhaling devices or nebulisers.

Asthma can be induced by agents to which a child is allergic such as pollens, mould, house dust and pets. Very occasionally food can cause an allergic reaction but more often it is the preservatives in the food such as tartrazine, sodium metabisulphite and monosodium glutamate that act as irritants. The most effective way of preventing all these reactions is obviously avoidance of the incriminating agents.

Epilepsy

As for asthma, this topic will not be discussed in great detail as it is the subject of another book specifically written for parents of children with epilepsy (see Further Reading).

Epilepsy is quite common, affecting about one in every 100 people. About 80 per cent of epilepsy commences in childhood or adolescence. There are numerous forms of epilepsy of which the commonest types include the following.

Grand Mal epilepsy: This is a major convulsion where the patient will lose control of the body, fall to the ground and jerk. Such convulsions may be quite brief, but may last for 20 to 30 minutes. The tongue may be bitten and the patient may pass urine during the fit. (The terms *fit, convulsion* and *seizure* all mean the same thing.) From a first aid point of view, the patient should be rolled onto the side with the head extended. Loosen any tight clothing around the neck and do not try to insert anything in the mouth. Contrary to popular belief, it is impossible to swallow one's tongue. Putting things in the mouth risks damaging the patient's teeth and your fingers may be badly bitten! If the fit lasts for more than five minutes, call for help or call an ambulance.

Petit Mal epilepsy (absences): This occurs in about five per cent of children with epilepsy and consists of brief interruptions of consciousness which usually last a few seconds. During these episodes the child is not 'with it' (absent) and stares vacantly into space. These episodes, which can occur a few, or many, times a day may be noticed by the parents, or the school teacher may notice that the child is not 'with it' during class. The diagnosis is relatively easy and the use of brain wave tests (the electro-encephalogram – EEG) is very helpful.

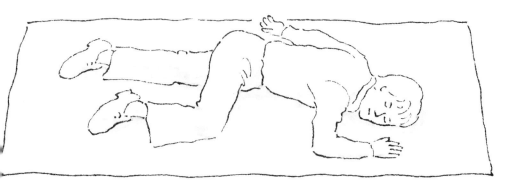

Recovery position for epilepsy

Temporal Lobe Epilepsy: This is a more complex form of epilepsy which may present with actual fits, prolonged absences or with some psychological features. Diagnosis is not always easy, even with modern techniques.

Treatment of epilepsy is with medication. About 70 per cent of people with epilepsy will have their fits well controlled with one medication alone. The outlook for most patients with epilepsy is very good indeed. Medications used in the treatment of epilepsy include carbamazepine (Tegretol, Convuline), sodium valproate (Epilim), phenytoin sodium (Epanutin), phenobarbitone or other barbiturates such as methylphenobarbitone (Prominal), clonazepam (Rivotril) or more recently clobazam (Frisium). All these agents may have side effects of some sort including drowsiness, weight gain, some effect on learning (barbiturates and phenytoin) and very rarely, liver damage (sodium valproate). Side effects should be fully explained to parents so that they can decide whether the improved control of seizures warrants persevering with the drugs and their side effects.

Diabetes

Diabetes is a condition which prevents the body from using glucose (a form of sugar) normally. This is because the pancreas does not produce enough insulin to allow the glucose to pass from the blood into the body tissues.

The treatment of diabetes in children includes giving insulin by injection, a special modified diet and exercise. It is also very helpful for children to learn as much as possible about their condition so that they can understand what is happening to them.

Diabetes education is better developed then epilepsy or asthma education in most countries. Interested readers should contact their local Diabetic Association.

10 Everyday maladies

Febrile convulsions

These are fits associated with fever. They are common, occurring in about four per cent of all children between the age of six months and five years. Febrile convulsions are very frightening for parents who may think that their child is dying. This is not the case; in fact febrile convulsions are essentially harmless and do not lead to later epilepsy.

There is nothing that can be done to prevent the first febrile convulsion as it is quite unexpected. About 30 per cent of children who have had one febrile convulsion will have another. This is where prevention is important. The most useful thing to do is to tackle the fever as soon as the child appears unwell, along the lines discussed in Chapter 7. This will often prevent the convulsion from occurring.

There is a small number of children who have recurrent febrile convulsions who may need treatment with an anti-fitting drug (anticonvulsant) such as phenobarbitone or who may require diazepam (Valium) given rectally when they have a fever and are liable to fit. This is very much the exception rather than the rule!

Headaches

Common causes of headache in children include tension headache, which we have all had from time to time, and 'attention' headache to draw attention to themselves. They hear adults talking of headache and getting sympathy; so, of course, they may imitate them. Bear in mind that visual problems may also be a cause of headache in school aged children. So it is wise to have their vision checked by an ophthalmologist or optometrist.

Migraine

Migraine headaches are also quite common in childhood, often occurring around puberty. They are probably due to some degree of spasm of the small arteries supplying the scalp and outer surface of the brain. Very occasionally headaches in children can be due to something more serious within the head, but this is very, very uncommon indeed.

As far as treatment is concerned, most mild headaches will wear off in a couple of hours without any medical treatment. Often parental interest and sympathy will do the trick. More severe or prolonged headaches can be dealt with as in adult life with paracetamol or aspirin. Migraine, if severe, may require the use of specific medications such as Migral, Deseril or Cafergot. Any headache which is persistent or unusually severe should be brought to the attention of your doctor.

Motion sickness

This problem seems to affect quite a lot of children, although some much more than others. It occurs during car trips, air travel and on the water. It usually gets better as the child gets older. There are lots of folk remedies for dealing with this problem and they are probably no better or worse than some of the medications available for preventing it. There is a whole range of remedies and your family chemist would be the best person to advise you.

Of particular interest is a new form of treatment presently being studied. This is the use of a drug called hyoscine, which has been used for a long time to treat motion sickness. It is presently being tried as a patch put onto the skin, so that the drug is absorbed through the skin into the body. The results have been good and this preparation is now on the market in Australia.

This being the case, treatment will be easy; you can simply apply the patch before a car trip and take it off afterwards!

11 Tummy troubles

The two most common problems which concern parents are constipation and diarrhoea, which have contrasting symptoms.

Constipation

This means the passage of hard motions (stools). It does not mean passing a stool every day or every other day. Anglo-Saxons are generally obsessed with their bowels and seem to believe that it is necessary to pass a motion daily at a fixed time to be in good health! Some people may only pass a stool every second, third or fourth day and may not be constipated. Constipation in children is very rarely due to any abnormality of the bowel (intestine). It may be related to difficult toilet training or more often a poor diet. You will have heard of dietary fibre, what our parents used to called roughage. Today's diet often contains little fibre. As a generalisation, the more processed or refined a food is, the less fibre it contains. Fibre comes from vegetables, fruit and cereals such as bran. A reasonable amount of these foods in the diet is usually all that is needed. Laxatives are rarely needed. Occasionally a child may become so constipated as to soil his/her pants; this is called encopresis. It occurs because the bowel is so full of motions that some leak out from the back passage (anus) from time to time. You should consult your doctor early on if this occurs.

Diarrhoea

Most children will have diarrhoea (which is a symptom of gastroenteritis) at some time or other, especially in the autumn or winter. It is often due to a viral infection, but may be due to contaminated food or drink. Most episodes only last a few days. The problem with diarrhoea is that the child loses a lot of fluid from the bowel and may become dehydrated. It is very important to maintain a high fluid intake even if the child is off his or her food.

Most children who are not vomiting profusely will take fluids by mouth very well even if they have to be given in small, frequent amounts. Rather than using the traditional flat lemonade, Lucozade and so on, it is better to give electrolyte solutions which contain some sodium and potassium, as well as sugar. These solutions are designed to allow the fluid taken by mouth to be well absorbed from the bowel. Recommended remedies, which come as powder sachets to be dissolved in water, such as Dioralyte and Electrosol, are available from your chemist. It is wise to have a sachet or two at home.

There is almost never any need for antibiotics by mouth in children with diarrhoea. In addition, medicines sold to stop diarrhoea are of little help and may be harmful. Medications used to stop vomiting, which are usually given by injection, are not to be recommended; they are of little value and may have side effects.

Tummy troubles

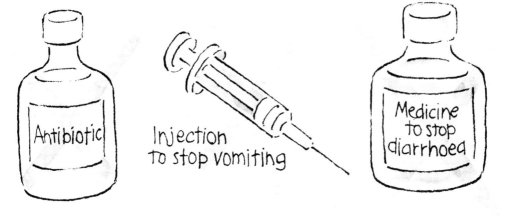

When can a solid diet be reintroduced?

Once the diarrhoea is beginning to improve, a solid diet can be reintroduced, usually after about 24 hours. In babies on milk there is no need to go through the time honoured ritual of giving ¼ strength milk, followed by ½ strength milk and so on. Simply go back on to a normal diet. This may induce the passage of a few extra loose stools but little else. Nor is there any need, in most cases, for the child to go onto a lactose free food such as a soya preparation or a specialised milk with no lactose such as Delact. This is only necessary if there is a condition known as lactose intolerance which only occurs after quite severe gastroenteritis. Lactose intolerance is associated with the passage of a lot of wind and loose, frothy stools. If this occurs, see your doctor.

Milk allergy

Milk allergy is much spoken about and is probably very rare. It can produce a rash, swelling of the body, especially the face and also diarrhoea. It is often 'diagnosed' with little evidence for its existence. The symptoms of milk allergy will disappear when milk is removed from the diet and very importantly will reoccur when milk is reintroduced, even in very small amounts. If this is a possibility in your child, you should consult a paediatrician or a paediatric allergist.

Dehydration

When babies in the first two months of life get diarrhoea, they are likely to get much sicker than older children and you should consult your doctor immediately. Young babies may get a generalised infection (septicaemia) in association with gastroenteritis and also the loss of fluid from the bowel may be quite extensive leading quickly to dehydration. In older children, the presence of blood in the stools is frightening and you should see your doctor if this occurs. In addition, if the child is quite unwell, unduly drowsy or dehydrated, you should seek medical assistance. Dehydration consists of a dry mouth, sunken eyes and listlessness. In young children, diarrhoea may be provoked by an associated infection in another part of the body such as the urinary tract or the middle ear. If there is such an associated infection, then antibiotics are appropriate. They are used to treat the associated infection, not the gastroenteritis itself.

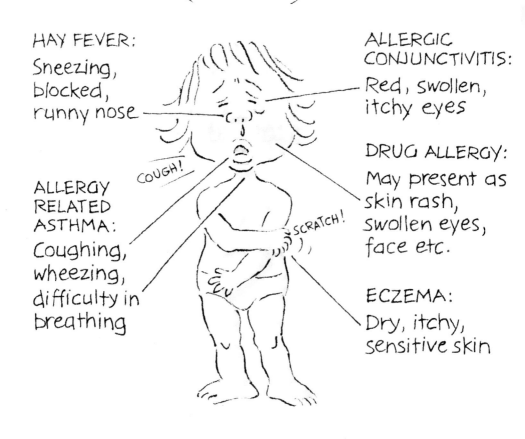

Allergy problems of childhood

12 Allergies

Allergic rhinitis

This condition may be seasonal, when it is called **hay fever**, or perennial when it occurs throughout the year. Perennial rhinitis is commoner than hay fever in children up to the teenage years. Hay fever is due to pollen allergy. The symptoms include a blocked and runny nose, sneezing and quite often snoring.

The most useful form of treatment for perennial rhinitis is the use of a topical steroid nasal spray such as Beconase. A useful treatment regime is one puff to each nostril three times a day for a week, one puff to each nostril twice daily for a second week and then one puff daily for about eight weeks. Antihistamines should not be used as they are of no value and may make the child drowsy or overexcited. Ordinary nose drops, especially those containing ephedrine (e.g. Neo-Synephrine) should not be used long term as they can alter the lining of the nose and leave it chronically damaged. It may be necessary to use such drops for up to a week at the beginning of treatment if the nose is very blocked.

Hay fever is also best treated locally either with a steroid spray or by inhaling sodium cromoglycate (Rynacrom) which is the same as Intal used in the treatment of asthma. Antihistamines may be of use, especially if the eyes are involved with conjunctivitis, redness, swelling and itch. In children, desensitization is very rarely indicated as it is potentially dangerous.

Allergic conjunctivitis

This is due to an allergic reaction in the conjunctiva, which is the outer lining of the eye. There is redness of the conjunctiva associated with swelling. The eyes are often itchy. This condition often occurs in association with allergic rhinitis. In mild cases, ordinary eye drops that you can obtain without prescription from your chemist will suffice. In more severe cases, it may be necessary to use steroid eye drops (e.g. Betnesol, Predsol or Maxidex) or sodium cromoglycate eye drops (Opticrom). Steroid drops should only be used under medical supervision.

Atopic dermatitis (Eczema)

The basic cause of the inflammation in this common condition is not understood. There is, however, certainly an allergic component, which may be associated with hay fever and asthma.

Eczema may begin at any age, but is visible by six months of age in about 75 per cent of those who are going to develop it. The skin is usually dry and itchy. In babies it affects mainly the cheeks and forehead; at the crawling stage mainly those areas of the legs and feet that are rubbed during crawling, whilst in the older child and adult it affects mainly skin creases at the elbows and knees.

It is important to realise that the skin dryness is a lifelong condition and that whilst the eczema will wax and wane, the skin always needs extra care. It is oversensitive and may react to substances which are not a problem for other people. Such irritants include wool, some types of nylon, some soaps, perfumed or medicated products, disinfectants and strong cleansers. Knowing which of these substances may be irritating for your child's skin is a matter of trial and error as they cannot all be avoided.

As far as treatment is concerned, it is important to concentrate on avoiding excessive skin dryness. This is best achieved by using a bath oil every day with a skin softener such as ten per cent glycerine in a sorbolene cream. Steroid creams or ointments are also very useful in localised areas or when the condition has flared up. There are many such preparations, for example Betnovate, but they should be used with great care and for short periods only.

Drug allergy

This occurs when a person is allergic to the constituents of a medication. This is a very individual thing and affects some people, but not others. Often the allergy appears as a skin rash which may be itchy or there may be swelling around the eyes, or of the face as a whole. This usually lasts a few days and then settles down spontaneously. There is usually no need to do anything about these reactions, except to avoid the drug in the future. Sometimes, if the itch is severe or the swelling uncomfortable or embarrassing, an antihistamine such as Phenergan may be useful. The drugs to which children are most often allergic are the penicillins like ampicillin, Amoxil etc.

Quite a lot of rashes are incorrectly labelled as being allergic. A child may contract a viral infection and develop a rash as part and parcel of the infection. If per chance the child is given a medication especially an antibiotic, it is likely that the antibiotic will be incorrectly blamed for the rash. A certain proportion of people who are labelled 'allergic to such and such' probably are not. Tests to unravel this predicament exist, but are complex and not without risk. So it is often easier to avoid that medication, unless it is essential, rather than undergo the tests.

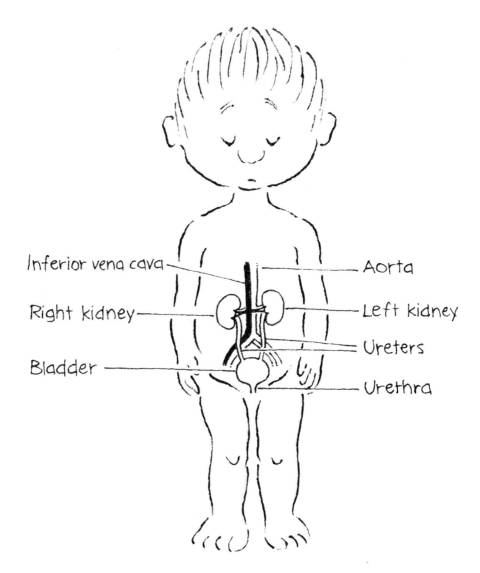

The urinary system

13 Urinary infections

Urinary infections are important not only in their own right, but also because a proportion of children who have a urinary infection may have an underlying abnormality of their urinary tract. The urinary tract consists of the kidneys, the ureters (which are the tubes connecting the kidneys to the bladder) the bladder itself and the urethra, the narrow tube which goes through the penis or into the vulva, through which we pass urine. Abnormalities of the urinary tract are anatomical in nature. For example there may be a double kidney on one side, or the ureter may enter the bladder abnormally. Such abnormalities hold up urine flow causing the urine to stagnate in the urinary tract and this may predispose it to infection. Children with such abnormalities are likely to have recurrent urinary infections and in such cases the urinary tract should be investigated as early as possible.

Symptoms of a urinary infection may include frequent passing of urine, a burning feeling when passing urine, wetting the bed, fever, pain in the loin, vomiting, diarrhoea and generally feeling unwell. The urine may be abnormally smelly and there may be blood visible in it.

When you take your child to the doctor with such symptoms, a specimen of urine will be collected and sent to the laboratory for analysis to prove whether or not the urine is actually infected. Sometimes it is difficult to obtain a clean specimen of urine from young children, especially girls. If several urine samples collected using a urine bag have been contaminated, your doctor may do what is called a 'bladder tap' (suprapubic aspiration of urine). This means putting a fine needle attached to a syringe through the tummy wall into the bladder. This always produces an uncontaminated sample. It is not a painful or frightening procedure and is done quite commonly in the young child so as to avoid getting a number of contaminated samples from urine bags.

What to do if your child has an infection

If an infection is found, then antibiotics are mandatory and MUST be taken for five to seven days. Antibiotics such as Amoxil, Septrin or Bactrim would usually be recommended. The antibiotics will kill off the infecting bacteria and it can be expected that the child will begin to feel better within a couple of days of commencing treatment. Despite the improvement, the course of antibiotics MUST be completed. If the infection is not controlled, so that it persists, kidney damage may occur. Once the infection has settled, repeated urine samples should be sent to the laboratory every few months for a year to make sure that all is well. In addition, because of the possibility of anatomical abnormalities of the urinary tract, all children who have a proven urinary infection should have a radiological (X-Ray) examination of their urinary tract. There are a number of ways of going about this and the tests include taking X-Rays of the kidneys (intravenous urography), injecting dye into the bladder to see if it goes backwards up the ureters (this is called ureteric reflux and does not happen very often), ultrasound of the kidneys and lastly some radioactive tests to examine the kidneys. Not all these tests are necessary in any one child and whichever one is done will depend on the suspected problem, the age of the child and the available tests in your area.

Ureteric reflux, which has already been mentioned, means that urine which normally comes down the ureter from the kidney, will be pushed back up the ureter when the child contracts his or her bladder when passing urine. This produces abnormal back pressure on the kidneys, and if the urine is infected, takes the infection up to the kidneys which therefore makes it undesirable. Reflux occurs in varying degrees of severity. In mild cases, nothing needs to be done, but severe reflux may need to be dealt with either by keeping the urine free from infection with long term antibiotics or sometimes by surgical means to correct the underlying abnormality.

It is important to understand what urinary tract infections are about and to deal with them promptly because of their possible long term effects. So don't hesitate to ask your doctor about anything you don't understand.

14 Hyperactivity

Hyperactivity is a condition which is of concern to many parents. The subject is surrounded by confusion and disagreement within the medical profession and others interested in the issue. There are difficulties in defining precisely what hyperactivity is, although typical symptoms include impulsive behaviour, poor concentration and a short attention span. However, there are no exact criteria for establishing the severity of the condition. A great deal of the information on hyperactivity is subjective and anecdotal.

Not surprisingly with such basic difficulties, there are no clear guidelines as to the correct treatment. Thus opinions vary between drug treatment with a medication such as Dexedrine, dietary management with the Feingold diet or some form of behavioural modification technique. All, or none, of these methods of management may work in individual children.

Prevention

15 Immunisation: so very important

What is immunisation?

Immunisation, or vaccination, as it is called by some, means building up antibodies to a bacterium or a virus so that the person who has been immunised will not get the disease, or at most will get it as a very mild illness. We talked earlier of antigen and antibody, with the antibody protecting you from an illness. That is what immunisation is all about. Take the measles vaccination for example. The measles virus (antigen) is grown in the laboratory in cell cultures of chick embryo and is then produced in such a way that it can be given to a child without causing measles. When the vaccine enters the body, antibodies are formed in the blood which prevent the child from getting measles when he or she encounters the measles virus in the community. This is the principle of all immunisations. **It is the only effective way to prevent infectious diseases.**

It might be expected that immunisation would be well accepted in the community and that all children would be fully immunised. This is not the case. In the UK, for example, 100,000 children a year get measles and 20 die. In 1982, 60,000 children got whooping cough and 13 died. This is quite unnecessary in this day and age.

Why aren't people immunised?

There are a number of reasons. For a start the present generation of parents have little experience of polio, diphtheria, measles, whooping cough and tetanus and think that they are trivial, mild or rare illnesses. Most people in their forties or fifties will have known someone who developed poliomyelitis and ended up partly paralysed; this would have motivated them to get their children vaccinated. Secondly, it is not always adequately explained by the medical profession that immunisation is not fool proof. If your child is vaccinated against measles, for example, it does not mean that there is 100 per cent protection. It means that there is a 90 to 95 per cent protection rate and those children who do get measles are likely to have a much milder illness. Thirdly there is an anti-vaccination lobby, led either by well meaning people whose children have had side effects from vaccination or the 'natural health' believers who see vaccination as some sort of assault on the individual, unproven and dangerous.

Side effects of immunisation

Last but not least, there is the problem of side effects. As we mentioned at the outset, all drugs have their side effects and vaccinations are no exception. It is important to get this into proportion and the facts should not be hidden, but openly discussed. No apologies are made for the facts and figures which follow; it is your right to know them!

Triple antigen

After triple antigen (diphtheria, tetanus and whooping cough) about 48 per cent of children will have a local reaction (redness, swelling or bruising at the site of injection), irritability and fever occurs in 40 per cent of recipients whilst seven per cent will scream persistently for hours. All these effects last a day or two.

The main concern with triple antigen is the risk of brain damage, which occurs in 1:310,000 recipients. But this is scarcely a greater risk than that of a child being drowned in a swimming pool or being injured crossing the road. The whooping cough component is believed to be responsible for these side effects and at present, major efforts are being made to purify the vaccine to avoid these problems. The only children who should not receive whooping cough vaccination are those who have a previous history of fits or brain damage, or those who have previously had a serious reaction to triple antigen.

Other vaccinations

Measles vaccination: This is very effective and its compulsory use in the USA to achieve school entry has reduced the number of cases of measles by 99 per cent. In Australia, where parents have been less concerned to have their children vaccinated, from 1967 to 1976, measles caused 111 deaths, more than diphtheria (11), whooping cough (18), tetanus (76) or polio (23).

Side effects from measles vaccination include a fever and a mild measles-like rash (five per cent), seven to ten days after the injection. There are no contraindications to measles vaccine in healthy children except perhaps egg allergy as the vaccine is grown in chick embryos. This should be discussed with your doctor.

Rubella (German measles) vaccination: This has been very successful in Australia. Rubella itself is a mild illness but it becomes dangerous if it is acquired in pregnancy when it can produce severe abnormalities in the developing baby. For this reason, vaccination is recommended for girls aged ten to thirteen years. Side effects may include a fever, sore throat, swollen glands, a mild rash and sometimes joint pains.

Hepatitis B vaccination: This has recently become available. It is expensive and in relatively short supply and should be only used in those at risk of getting hepatitis. In childhood this would include those children who receive blood transfusions, such as haemophiliacs, and newborn babies whose mothers are carriers of the virus.

Tetanus immunisation: This is given as part of the triple antigen and is the only way of eradicating tetanus in the community. If an injury is sustained, a booster dose should be given if the last injection was given more than three to five years previously.

Poliomyelitis vaccination is given by mouth. There is a very small risk that if parents or others in the family have not been immunised, they could be infected by the child who has just had the vaccination; ideally they should be immunised at the same time. One in four million children receiving polio vaccination may develop polio.

The present immunisation recommendations for the UK are shown in the table on page 99.

In summary, every immunisation carries a risk. This has to be balanced between the extremely small risk of modern immunisation and the much more serious risk of contracting the illness. The risk is small and immunisation is vital for your child and for the community at large.

Recommended immunisation schedule (1987)

Age	Disease	Vaccine
2 Months	Diphtheria, tetanus, pertussis (whooping cough), Poliomyelitis	Triple vaccine (DTP) Sabin vaccine
4 Months	As above	As above
6 Months	As above	As above
12-24 Months	Measles	Measles
5 years (before school entry)	Diphtheria, tetanus, polio	Combined diphtheria and tetanus (CDT) Sabin
10-13 years (Females only)	Rubella (German measles)	Rubella
15 years or before leaving school	Poliomyelitis, tetanus	Sabin, tetanus (ADT)

6 Vitamins: who needs them?

The popular press is full of articles on vitamins which are meant to pep us up, prevent colds and generally solve most problems. Every year millions are spent by the general public on vitamins, most of which are not needed by the body and are excreted in the urine. The concentration of vitamins in the sewage system must be tremendous!!

What are vitamins?

They are a group of chemical compounds which occur in minute amounts in foods. There are 13 vitamins which are required by the human body and they are essential for growth and reproduction.

Vitamin A: This is essential for the eyes to adjust to various light intensities. Deficiency leads to night blindness and eye damage.

Vitamin B: This is a group of vitamins, B_1 – thiamine, B_2 – riboflavin, B_3 – niacin or nicotinic acid and B_6 – pyridoxine. These vitamins are intimately involved with the cellular workings of the body and the release of energy from a lot of the foods that we eat. Deficiency of thiamine leads to beri beri, riboflavin deficiency produces dermatitis and cracking of the lips and corners of the mouth, niacin deficiency produces pellagra whilst pyridoxine deficiency can produce fits in newborn infants, anaemia and disorders of the nervous system. Folic acid and vitamin

B_{12} have important functions in chemical processes within the body and help produce healthy blood cells.

Vitamin C: This is a powerful reducing substance and helps to hold the body's cells together. Deficiency leads to scurvy.

Vitamin D: This controls how the body handles calcium and phosphorus and deficiency produces rickets.

Vitamin E: Precisely what this does is uncertain as are the symptoms of deficiency although blood problems in premature infants have been described.

With the push to take more and more vitamins, the question that needs to be asked is how much do we need? Standards have been developed by many organisations including the World Health Organisation and they have defined the recommended daily allowances (RDA) for vitamins and other food stuffs. **The RDA for vitamins is achieved by virtually all Westerners every day on a normal diet, even with a fair amount of 'junk food'.**

Who may need extra vitamins?

During infancy, with rapid growth, Vitamin D may require supplementation especially in premature infants. But do take advice from your doctor since vitamins A and D are potentially **fatal** in overdose, especially in children. Other situations liable to cause relative deficiency include pregnancy, old age, alcoholism and malnutrition. Besides these situations there is really no need to provide extra vitamins.

What then of the claims that huge doses of vitamins (megadoses) help to maintain and enhance health? These claims have been made for curing the common cold, cancer, arthritis and heart disease. It is also claimed that megavitamins may combat fatigue, alleviate impotence and enhance athletic performance. However, much as it may raise the ire of practitioners of megadose treatment, it has to be said that there is no good scientific evidence that any of these treatments are of any use. As we have discussed before, all drugs and chemical agents have side effects and vitamins are no exception, particularly high doses of vitamins. Certainly some people who have taken megadose vitamins have got better. However they may have got better anyway or it may be related to what is called a placebo effect, which means having faith in getting better from whatever you might be taking. The placebo effect is a very real phenomenon which has not been adequately tested in the field of megadose vitamins.

The use of vitamin tonics for children is of little value, but probably does equally little harm. Perhaps another placebo effect.

It is exceedingly rare to see any patients with frank vitamin deficiency, which is a reflection of an adequate diet and not any supplementary vitamins that might have been taken.

Epilogue

Ah the paradise that awaits us in 1984! For every ill a pill. Tranquillizers to overcome angst, pep pills to wake us up, life pills to ensure blissful sterility. I will lift mine eyes unto the pills whence my help cometh.

Malcolm Muggeridge

There are no really safe drugs, only safe physicians.

H. A. Kaminetsky

These two quotations reflect the reality of over prescribing, albeit more in adult practice than for children, and they serve as a reminder that all drugs have the potential to produce side effects. The only way to avoid side effects is not to take the medication in the first place.

Taking medication should be a balanced decision, a cost benefit analysis, between the severity of the illness and the risk of side effects. This is a decision which should be reached between doctor and parent(s).

The purpose of this book is to give you, as parents, some background, factual information which you can use when discussing medications with your doctor or pharmacist. It is not a comprehensive encyclopaedia, but has highlighted the common conditions seen in community paediatric practice.

As patients, you and your children have the right to information about your health and any medications or tests suggested by your doctor. Having rights also implies responsibilities. In the final analysis your health is your responsibility, as is your children's health. Your doctor cannot lead your life for you, but is there to help and advise. It is hoped that the information in this book may allow you to discuss child health matters more easily with your doctor. Don't be embarrassed to ask questions or arrive at the surgery with questions written as a little shopping list. If your questions are not answered to your satisfaction, obtain a second opinion.

Please glance at the question and answer section and the list of drugs commonly used in children, which follow in this book.

Appendices

1 Some questions that parents might ask

My son, who is four years old, has had two bouts of tonsillitis and an ear infection, this past year. My doctor has suggested a tonsillectomy may be beneficial. Is this likely?

The suggested indications for tonsillectomy are discussed in Chapter 8. Your son has really not had enough episodes of tonsillitis to consider tonsillectomy. Moreover, as he gets older he will have fewer infections and thus is likely to improve anyway.

I find it difficult to ask my doctor questions about the children's health, he's always so busy.

There may be a number of problems. You may be leaving your questions until the end of the consultation when your doctor expects you to be leaving so that he or she can see the next patient. Try asking earlier on.

You may not be expressing yourself very clearly. If you get flustered in this situation, write down your questions on a bit of paper and ask them one by one. Sometimes your doctor may be a poor communicator; not all doctors express themselves well. If this is the case, and you do not feel that your questions are being answered to your satisfaction, it may be appropriate to seek a doctor to whom you can speak to more easily.

My son, who is aged three, seems to be on antibiotics almost all of the time. No sooner is he over one infection, than he gets another and some more antibiotics. Surely this can't be any good for him?

This is a very common parental concern. As discussed in Chapter 1, most children will, under normal circumstances, have a lot of infections during their early childhood. This is quite normal; it is part of growing up. A good proportion of these infections will be viral and so do not require treatment with antibiotics. However, as discussed in Chapter 6, it is impractical to differentiate between bacterial and viral infections in everyday practice. It is too complicated and expensive. So to cover all eventualities, antibiotics are prescribed.

It is quite common to have a parent tell the doctor that their child had a viral infection, but as soon as they started the antibiotics, the child got better. This only means that the child was going to get better anyway. Don't forget that in the days before antibiotics, not all that long ago, children recovered from tonsillitis, otitis media and so on. This is not to suggest that antibiotics are of no value and should not be used, just that children often get well of their own accord.

If you as a parent feel that your child is getting too much in the way of medication, ask your doctor about it and if necessary get a referral to a paediatrician. Do not be put down because you are simply a parent; as a profession we have become rather bad at recognising parental intuition which we tend to pooh pooh. A silly mistake on our part.

My chemist has suggested that I give my six year old son who has a recurrent cough some cough medicine. He has been taking it for two weeks now with no effect. What should I do next?

Firstly, you should bear in mind that a recurrent cough may be the only symptom of asthma. You should have your child looked at from this point of view. A general examination of the chest, ears and throat is called for.

In general, cough medicines (suppressants) are of little value. They are all designed to suppress (damp down) the cough. If there is a chest infection, this is the wrong thing to do as to clear the chest, the phlegm (sputum) must be coughed up. Suppressing the cough in this situation is counterproductive. If the cough is coming purely from the throat, most cough medicines may produce some very temporary relief, but probably not very much more than soothing the throat with a warm drink!!

My son aged five years has had several fits; grand mal they were called. He was started on phenobarbitone. Since then he has become very hyperactive and aggressive. What can I do about it?

The story that you give is not uncommon. Somewhere between 20 and 40 per cent of children who receive phenobarbitone for the treatment of epilepsy, or the prevention of febrile convulsions will develop hyperactive behaviour. This varies a great deal in severity and the only way to stop it is to come off the medication and change to something else.

My son, aged six years, is hyperactive. He never stands still, is always on the move and never has time to concentrate on any one thing. I have read a lot about hyperactivity and its various treatments. What is the role of medication such as Dexedrine?

The answer to this question is not fully understood. Dexedrine is a stimulant, but in hyperactive children is claimed to have a calming effect. Quite why is uncertain.

There are a lot of problems in the study of hyperactivity which make answers hard to come by. Just the very definition of hyperactivity is difficult. How much activity is hyperactive? You will appreciate that at the end of the day when you have come in from work or have been busy in the house all day, that even a fairly normally behaved youngster may seem hyperactive. That is because you feel weary and jaded and any movement around you is too much to bear.

With this confusion in trying to define hyperactivity, it is hardly surprising that a lot of the studies which have been done on various suggested treatments have not produced any very useful results. To make things worse, the area is a very emotional one. There are those who believe, come what may, in dietary management. Others believe in medication and yet others believe that the condition will get better whatever is done about it and so on. All these beliefs are held with great conviction, almost invariably based on no good evidence other than personal experience or some or other anecdote.

What is Dexedrine? Is this of any use in hyperactivity? What is known is that Dexedrine will improve short term attention span and impulsivity, but seems to have no effect on longer term concentration. It is also uncertain as to whether it has any beneficial effects on hyperactivity itself. The concern about Dexedrine, is that it is a powerful stimulant of the brain that may be being used in children with growing brains, when there is little evidence that it is of any value.

As we discussed before, taking any medication implies a balance between benefit from the drug and any possible side effects. If the benefit is great and the side effects few, then that is fine. The reverse would be unacceptable. **In the case of Dexedrine, the benefits are dubious and the side effects of long term exposure uncertain.** If I were a gambling man, I'm not sure that I would take a punt on it!!

My son aged eight, wets the bed several nights a week. My doctor has suggested using some medication called Tofranil. Does it work and is it safe?

Bedwetting (enuresis) is not an uncommon problem. It is important to make sure that it is not a symptom of a urinary tract infection (Chapter 13). Having excluded this, then there are three main ways of managing the problem which include:

- Behavioural techniques using gold stars on charts and other rewards for dry nights.

- A bell and pad technique. When the child first passes a drop of urine in the bed, it lands on the pad which sets off the bell and wakes the child. He is then meant to go to the toilet and empty his bladder. This again is a behavioural modification technique.

- Tofranil, which is used for the treatment of depression in adults, is said to help a proportion of children with enuresis. How this medication works in this condition is quite unknown. In general its side effects are few and it may help in a proportion of patients.

The management of enuresis, like that of hyperactivity, is ensconced in folklore and myth. Studies are difficult to do well and thus the situation remains confused.

My child of nine months of age sleeps poorly at night, often waking several times during the night. We haven't had a full night's sleep for several months and are at the end of our tether. Is there anything that can be done?

This again is a not uncommon story from parents. Little is known about sleep patterns, especially disturbed sleep patterns, in infancy. So whatever is suggested by your doctor is usually based on experience rather than any great scientific truth. This does not make it any worse, but it suggests that you are likely to get as many opinions as doctors and nurses whom you might ask.

My own suggestion, based purely on experience, is that it may be of value to give the child sleeping medication for a week to two weeks to try and break the 'non sleeping cycle'. If this works, it allows everyone to get some rest and that in itself makes the situation more tolerable. I would anticipate that this would work in about 50 to 70 per cent of children in this situation.

There are two main groups of drugs which can be used for this sort of sedation. The first is the chloral group of drugs e.g. Noctec, Triclofos Elixir etc or the antihistamines such as Vallergan or Phenergan. I personally do not like the antihistamines for sedation, as it is not uncommon for them to produce some overactivity as well as nightmares. Overall, a chloral preparation, in my opinion, is more suitable. Use it only for a week or two and only under medical supervision.

My daughter who is three months old had a fever of 39°C after her first triple antigen shot and cried a lot. Should she have the remaining two injections?

As discussed in Chapter 15, this sort of reaction is not uncommon and is harmless. On balance, the benefits of immunisation very greatly outweigh the possible side effects. There should be no problem in your going ahead with your daughter's course of immunisations.

Once again the subject of complications of immunisation, especially brain damage, is a very emotive one. Whilst it is appreciated with great sympathy the difficulties suffered by the families of children who have had these side effects, it must be remembered that they are extremely uncommon. The benefits of eradicating childhood infectious illnesses must, for society as a whole, outweigh the complications which occur.

My baby boy is two months old and gets a lot of colic. What can be done about it?

Firstly, the cause of colic is not understood. The baby appears to be in pain, will stiffen up and often draw his or her legs up towards his tummy. It is assumed that this is due to wind in the bowel, although this has never been proven. Whatever the cause, colic disappears over the first six months of life.

This is of little consolation to the mother who is often very distraught and short of sleep. What can be done about it? Probably the most effective form of 'treatment' is movement; bouncing or rocking the baby, patting the baby's back and so on. There used to be a medication Merbentyl, used in the treatment of colic but this is no longer recommended for use under the age of one year because of possible side effects relating to breathing. There is really nothing else that is suitable.

My daughter aged 11 is lethargic and seems run down. Would it be of help for her to take some extra vitamins?

As discussed in Chapter 16, most people in the western world on an adequate diet, have no need for extra vitamins. They receive plenty in an average diet. It would be better for your daughter to see your doctor and have a full physical check up to assure yourself that there is nothing wrong.

My two year old son sucks his thumb. Is this normal?

Thumb sucking is a very common habit amongst young children; so common as to be regarded as normal. Most children stop sucking their thumbs by three to four years of age. It does not damage the shape of the permanent teeth and is a harmless pastime. It is most often seen when children are tired, bored, stressed or going off to sleep. Thumb sucking seems to be a comforter for some children.

I would like to have my six month old son circumcised. I cannot pull back his foreskin to clean him up and anyway all the men in the family have been circumcised. When I talked to my doctor about this, she said it was not a good idea. Why?

It is important to understand that it is normal for the foreskin not to be able to be pulled back in the first two years of life. This serves a protective function and protects the end of the penis (the glans) from being burnt and ulcerated from urine in wet nappies. Any attempt to pull the foreskin back in the very young child will lead to tears between the foreskin and the penis and this may lead to a situation where it cannot be pulled back at all in later life.

Indications for circumcision include:

- Phimosis, which means a very tight foreskin, so tight that there may be difficulties in passing urine.

- Balanitis, which means an infection of the foreskin.

- Ritual or religious reasons.

- Psychological reasons in older children, adolescents or adults.

My two month old baby has 'clicky hips'. Does this mean that they are dislocated?

Every child should be examined at birth for the presence of dislocated hips which occurs in about four out of every 1000 babies. Quite a lot of babies will have clicky hips, but this does not necessarily mean that they are dislocated. If the hips are dislocated, it will not be possible to turn the thighs outwards. 'Clicky hips' as such are just an indication for a monthly review. Some doctors may suggest putting double nappies on the baby just for a bit more support. There is little purpose in doing X-Rays of the hips in the first three months of life as the top of the femur (the thigh bone) is not developed and cannot be seen on X-Ray.

2 Common medicines used in childhood

As mentioned previously, fewer medicines are used in childhood than in adults. This section of the book will provide some information on commonly used medications, what they are used for, their side effects and so on. Drugs are listed in alphabetical order using their trade names. Again it is not meant to be comprehensive and will only cover some drugs in common use. Inclusion of a particular medication, or brand of medication, in this list, has no implication as to its superiority over any equivalent medication. See the section on further reading for more information.

Actifed: An over-the-counter antihistamine which is recommended for nasal and respiratory tract congestion, i.e. the common cold, hay fever etc. May cause drowsiness and in some children, overactivity. Antihistamines act by reducing inflammation and drying up secretions.

Amoxil: This is the trade name for amoxycillin, one of the broad spectrum penicillins (see Chapter 6) which are used for the treatment of many infections, both minor and major. Unlike most other medications, it may be preferable to take Amoxil on an empty stomach. Side effects include an allergic rash and sometimes diarrhoea. Prolonged use may be associated with the development of thrush in the mouth.

Ascabiol: This is a liquid preparation of benzyl benzoate which is applied to the skin to treat scabies (caused by mites). This drug works by a direct action on the parasites in the skin.

Bactrim: This is a combination antibiotic which contains two active agents which when combined are known as cotrimoxazole. It has a broad spectrum action against many bacteria. Side effects are relatively few and consist of tummy upsets and very rarely some changes in the platelet component of the blood.

Beconase nasal spray: This is a topical corticosteroid preparation which is particularly useful in the treatment of hay fever. This drug, like all steroid medications, reduces inflammation and this is how it works on hay fever.

Becotide inhaler: This inhaled corticosteroid preparation is used in the prevention and treatment of asthma. Because it is inhaled, little enters the bloodstream and thus there are very few side effects.

Becotide rotacaps: A variant of the Becotide inhaler. Some children find this easier to use than the inhaler.

Benadryl: Another antihistamine. Comments as for Actifed.

Calpol: A product containing paracetamol, useful in the management of pain and fever. The side effects of paracetamol in childhood are absolutely negligible. Paracetamol has an effect on that part of the brain which controls body temperature.

Cerumol: This is used for loosening wax in the ears. Insert five drops in each ear, and then, at least in principle, the wax should be easily removed with a cotton wool bud after about half an hour.

Combantrin: This is used in the treatment of threadworm, roundworm and hookworms. Considered very safe.

Dioctyl: A laxative.

Dioralyte: This is a salt (electrolyte) product, which, when made up with water in the correct proportions, is used in the treatment of gastroenteritis (See Chapter 11).

Erythromycin: This is an antibiotic which is useful in treating Gram positive organisms. It is quite frequently used in people who are, or are said to be, allergic to penicillin as it will not cause allergy in them. It should not be used in combination with theophylline in the treatment of asthma or carbamazepine in the treatment of epilepsy as it blocks the breakdown of these two agents in the body and leads to toxicity.

Erythrocin: As for Erythromycin.

Flagyl: Used in the treatment of an intestinal parasite called Giardia, which may cause recurrent diarrhoea in children. This drug has a direct effect on Giardia, killing the parasites.

Furadantin: This is a urinary antibacterial medication containing nitrofurantoin. May be used in urinary tract infections. Side effects are few, but the urine may become yellow-brown in colour while on this medication. Parents and children should be warned of this.

Hibitane: Contains the antiseptic chlorhexidine. Extensively used in many households as a concentrated liquid, lozenges or cream.

Ilosone: See Erythromycin.

Imodium: This is used in the treatment of diarrhoea. As mentioned in Chapter 11 there is really no need to give such agents to children with diarrhoea, as it is a self limiting illness. However this agent does appear to work with minimal side effects. It may occasionally be indicated for use in childhood and acts by reducing the irritability and movement of the bowel.

Intal: A very useful agent which can be inhaled and is used for the prevention of asthma. It has no side effects to speak of. Intal acts by stabilising the chemical systems in the airways (bronchi).

Keflex: One of the broad spectrum antibiotics of the cephalosporin group of which there are many examples. May produce some diarrhoea after prolonged or recurrent courses.

Lomotil: Used in the treatment of diarrhoea. Best not used in children as side effects, which include blurred vision, dry mouth and later abnormalities of the nervous system, are quite common. It is reasonably effective, but in children, especially young children, side effects outweigh the benefits. It acts by slowing down bowel movements.

Noctec: Contains chloral hydrate which is extensively used in children to make then sleep. Side effects are very few indeed. Chloral hydrate itself has a quite repulsive taste, but most commercially available preparations are quite palatable. Another brand name is Triclofos Elixir.

Nuelin SA: Contains theophylline, which is one of the mainstays of the management of asthma. Available as a liquid preparation, tablets and slow release tablets. Side effects include nausea, vomiting, tremulousness and agitation. Theophylline has a number of actions in the body. The most important action in asthma is to relax the muscular component of the airways (bronchi). This allows the bronchi to widen and air to be breathed out more easily.

Nystatin: Available as a suspension, tablets or as a cream. Used for the treatment of candidal infection, (thrush). Candida is a fungal infection and nystatin has a direct effect on the fungus.

Panadol: Available as a liquid preparation, drops, tablets and suppositories. As for Calpol.

Penbritin: This is the broad spectrum antibiotic ampicillin. Comments as for Amoxil.

Periactin: An antihistamine. Comments as for Actifed.

Phenergan: An antihistamine. Comments as for Actifed.

Phensedyl: Combination of Phenergan with a cough suppressant, Pholcodine and a decongestant. Occasionally of use in childhood.

Rynacrom capsules: (for insufflation) Inhaled into the nose. Useful in the management of hay fever. No side effects to speak of. This drug is similar to Intal and acts in the same way.

Septrin: Different trade name for the same basic compound as Bactrim.

Stemetil: Used to counteract nausea and vomiting. Not recommended in children unless essential, as side effects similar to those described for Lomotil, are common.

TheoDur: Similar to slow release Nuelin.

Tixylix: Contains an antihistamine, a cough suppressant and a decongestant. Quite often recommended for night time cough.

Vermox: Used in the treatment of pinworms, roundworms, whipworms, threadworms and hookworms. Side effects may include tummy pain, nausea, vomiting, headache or drowsiness. This drug acts directly on the worms and kills them.

3 What to keep in the medicine cabinet

A medicine cabinet should be practical and not contain too many items. Keeping unlabelled or outdated medications in the medicine cabinet is a very dangerous practice and should be avoided at all costs. As a general guide the following items would be useful to have on hand:

- Regular medications which a family member is taking, such as for asthma or epilepsy

- Paracetamol (preferably as a liquid) such as Panadol or Calpol for fever, headaches, aches and pains

- Antiseptic cream such as Savlon or Dettol for cuts and bites

- Calamine lotion for insect bites

- Surgical spirit for cleaning wounds

- Sticking plasters, cotton wool, crepe and gauze bandages, a triangular bandage, blunt ended scissors, safety pins, and blunt ended tweezers for cuts, scratches, bruises, sprains, splinters and possible fractures.

4 Useful addresses

Asthma Society and Friends of the Asthma Research Council
300 Upper Street
London N1 2XX

01-226 2260

National Society for Epilepsy
Chalfont Centre for Epilepsy
Chalfont St Peter
Buckinghamshire

02407-3991

Health Education Council
78 New Oxford Street
London WC1

01-631 0930

Hyperactive Children's Support Group
59 Meadowside
Angmering
Littlehampton
Sussex BN16 4BW

5 Further reading

Belinda Barnes and Irene Colquhoun **The Hyperactive Child: What the Family Can Do** Thorsons, 1984.

Neil Buchanan **Childhood Asthma** Piatkus, 1987.

Chadwick and Usiskin **Living With Epilepsy** Dunitz, 1987.

Adelle Davis **Let's Have Healthy Children** Unwin Paperbacks, 1968.

P. Dreisbach and W. Robertson **Handbook of Poisoning: Prevention, Diagnosis and Treatment** Academic Press, 1987.

J. W. Farquhar **The Diabetic Child** Churchill Livingstone, Third Edition, 1981.

Dorothy Francis **Nutrition For Children** Blackwell Scientific Publications, 1986.

Christopher Green **Toddler Taming** Century, 1984.

Diana Hastings **The Macmillan Guide to Home Nursing** Macmillan, 1986.

Hopkins **Epilepsy: The Facts** Oxford Paperbacks, 1984.

Illingworth **Infections — and Immunisation of Your Child** Churchill Livingstone.

Richard Lechtenberg **Epilepsy and The Family** Harvard University Press, 1984.

Peter Mansfield and Jean Monro **Chemical Children — How to Protect Your Family from Harmful Pollutants** Century, 1987.

A. D. Milner **Asthma in Childhood** Churchill Livingstone, 1984.

Peter Parish **Medicines — A Guide for Everybody** Penguin, Fifth Edition 1985.

Tony Smith (ed.) **Family Doctor Home Adviser** Dorling Kindersley, 1986.

Eric Taylor **The Hyperactive Child** Dunitz, 1985.

Diana Wells **Daniel: Living With an Allergic Child** Ashgrove Press, 1985.

Miriam Wood **Living with a Hyperactive Child** Souvenir Press, 1984.